THE UNOFFICIAL HARRY POTTER INSULTS HANDBOOK

Join us online at **www.HarryPotterInsults.com.**

THE UNOFFICIAL HARRY POTTER INSULTS HANDBOOK

A VERY SPECIAL THANKS TO COVER AND LAYOUT DESIGNER CODY WELLONS AND ILLUSTRATOR STERLING MARTIN. WE MUST HAVE BEEN DRINKING FELIX FELICIS THE DAY YOU TALENTED MEN AGREED TO HELP WITH THIS PROJECT. THANK YOU!

THE UNOFFICIAL HARRY POTTER INSULTS HANDBOOK

TESTIMONIALS

"This book gave me the confidence to stand up for myself.
Now if only they'd make a book that would teach me how to
pull my wand out of my nose."
–BRYAN BIGGLES, HUFFLEPUFF

"I used to spend every afternoon crying in the bathroom with Moaning
Myrtle, but things changed after I armed myself with these insults.
I haven't been bullied in over a year! This is the best book in the world!*"
–MRS. H. PERBOLEE, HUFFLEPUFF

"Peeves stole this book from me while I was in Potions class.
Now he's worse than ever."
–YOLANDA PERKINS, RAVENCLAW

"This handbook would really help my brother who gets wedgies every
day. After I read it a few more times, maybe I'll pass it along to him."
–SANDY SPROUTSWORTH, RAVENCLAW

"Before this guide, I was the butt of every Slytherin joke.
But after reading it, I feel like a true Gryffindor!"
–NEVILLE LONGBOTTOM, GRYFFINDOR

"This book has ruined my life. Now I'm the one who gets picked on."
– KEVIN CURDS, SLYTHERIN

This statement has not been verified by the Ministry of Magic.

INTRODUCTION

Are you tormented in Transfiguration?
Are you mocked for your muggle mum?
Do you long for a Time-Turner so you can always deliver
a killer comeback?

Whether you're a N.E.W.T.-level wizard
or a wide-eyed witch still awaiting your
Hogwarts acceptance letter, you've probably encountered
a merciless Malfoy or despicable Dursley who makes your
magical blood boil. If you've ever stood speechless as someone
called you a talentless squib, a worthless git or a filthy
mudblood, this is the book for you!

Study these magical pages closely, and with a little
Hufflepuff hard work you'll soon brave any bully
with the courage of a Gryffindor and be able to outwit even
the smartest Ravenclaw or the most cunning Slytherin!

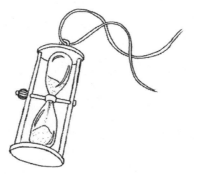

REPEAT
AFTER ME...

I SOLEMNLY SWEAR TO USE THIS BOOK FOR GOOD.

YOUR OWL IS LAME!

HISTORY OF THE MAGICAL BULLY

Bullies have existed in the magical world for as long as magic itself has been around. Indeed, even young witches and wizards of prehistoric times had to contend with magical menaces who transfigured innocent witches into woolly mammoths and used their wands to aim wind up the loincloths of unsuspecting wizards.

However, it wasn't until the year 1000 A.D. that we find our first well-documented case of a wizard bully — none other than Salazar Slytherin himself. It was around this time that Slytherin and three other great witches and wizards of the age — Godric Gryffindor, Helga Hufflepuff and Rowena Ravenclaw — decided to form Hogwarts School of Witchcraft and Wizardry. Disagreements over what kind of students should be allowed to study at the school are what led to some of the first instances of magical bullying.

It all started when Slytherin, tired of Hufflepuff's never-ending attempts to mediate the foursome's disagreements, performed a switching spell and replaced Hufflepuff's sugar with salt. Naturally, this little prank resulted in a very bad cup of tea — and Gryffindor's using a Hurling Hex to throw the tea into Slytherin's face. At this point, Ravenclaw intervened and suggested that Hogwarts admit only those students with the greatest intellectual potential, so Slytherin silenced her with a wave of his wand and told her that her diadem made her look fat. From this point on, Slytherin became a relentless bully — calling his colleagues names, cursing them whenever they turned their backs and repeatedly threatening them with the monster he claimed to have hidden in Hogwarts.

Perhaps the next most-famous incidents of magical bullying occurred in 1689 immediately following the signing of the International Statute of Wizarding Secrecy. Ironically, the statute was introduced to end the widespread persecution of wizarding children by muggles, but resulted in extensive muggle-baiting and bullying. In fact, according to ancient wizarding texts, the first recorded instance of a shrinking key occurred just a year later in 1690.

As you know, bullies still walk the halls of magical education institutions from the icy mountains surrounding Durmstrang to the balmy beaches outside Beauxbatons. And, of course, Hogwarts has its share of bullies too. While Slytherin House continues to produce the greatest number of belligerent bullies — namely, the terrible You-Know-Who — they're not exclusive to this house. Ravenclaw has been known to house a number of hostile know-it-alls, a handful of Gryffindors have used their courage for less-then-honorable means, and even Hufflepuff has produced a not-so-friendly witch. Indeed, even some of those wizards we hold in high regard today — including Harry Potter's own godfather, Sirius Black — had a sordid history of bullying in their past.

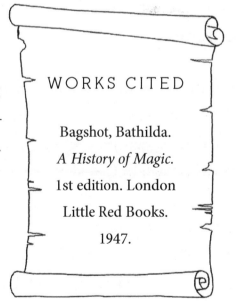

WORKS CITED

Bagshot, Bathilda.
A History of Magic.
1st edition. London
Little Red Books.
1947.

QUIT HITTING YOURSELF

The halls of Hogwarts can be intimidating for even the most courageous of Gryffindors. A student's education in the wonders of wizardry is filled with perils — from advanced Potions to Defense Against the Dark Arts — and every legendary wizard has confronted a dreaded wand-yielding roughneck. Harry Potter battled He-Who-Must-Not-Be-Named, the greatest magical bully of our time — and that's not all. Harry faced other rude ruffians, including Acromantulas, Whomping Willows, Malfoys, Basilisks, Lestranges, trolls and horcruxes, just to name a few. And while Harry sometimes felt he wasn't good enough to take on all these magical menaces, he pulled himself up by his robestraps and found the confidence he needed to defeat some of the worst bullies ever. Even Ron Weasley, Harry's skittish best friend, was able to summon Gryffindor's courage to vanquish his worst enemies. So don't worry! This handbook is here to help you become a confident, fearless wizard who can dish out the snappiest insults to the worst of Hogwarts' hooligans. Quit hitting yourself! You're going to be a great wizard. Just wait and see...

Wizards bullied BEFORE reading this book.

80%

Wizards bullied AFTER reading this book

2%

*Still doubting yourself? Don't! Believe it or not, some of the most celebrated sorcerers in history were also the victims of belligerent bullies! Keep an eye out for Famous Wizard Insults cards to learn more about these historically humiliated witches and wizards.

WAYS TO IDENTIFY A MAGICAL BULLY

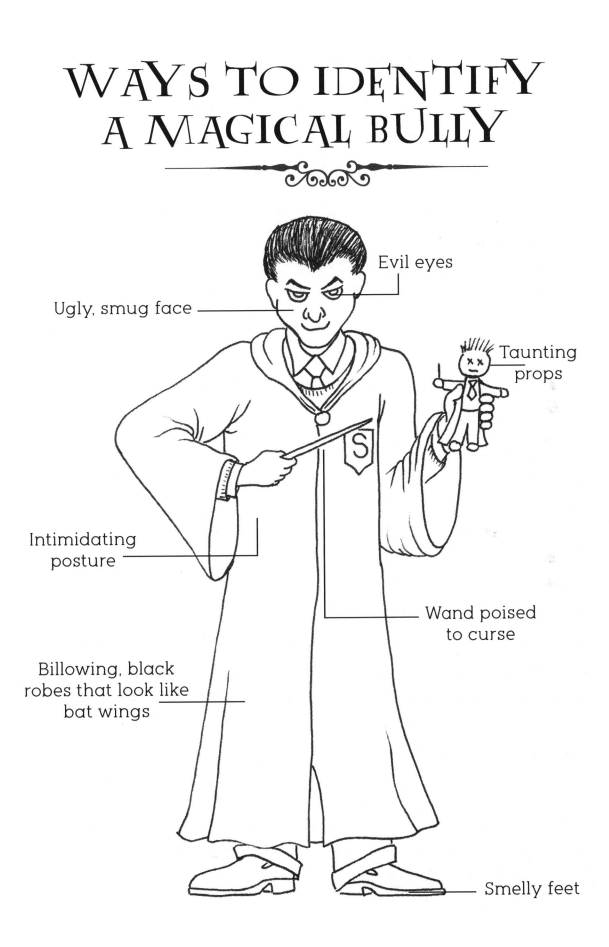

Evil eyes

Ugly, smug face

Taunting props

Intimidating posture

Wand poised to curse

Billowing, black robes that look like bat wings

Smelly feet

TIPS FOR A SUCCESSFUL DELIVERY

These diagrams will show you the correct and incorrect ways to execute a cutting comeback. If you follow the advice on these drawings, you'll have great success at delivering magical insults!

THE WRONG WAY

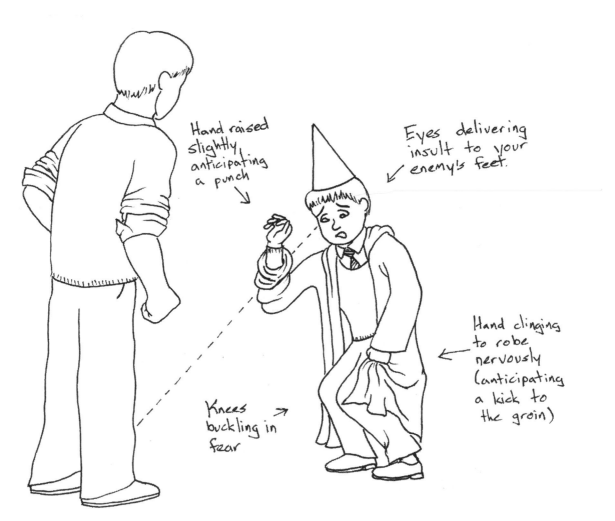

Hand raised slightly, anticipating a punch

Eyes delivering insult to your enemy's feet.

Hand clinging to robe nervously (anticipating a kick to the groin)

Knees buckling in fear

THE RIGHT WAY

See the difference? Confidence really goes a long way.

A TEST TO BEGIN ALL TESTS

Before you begin your education in magical insults, take this quiz to assess whether you're a Spineless Sorcerer, a Wand-Happy Wizard or something in between.

1. You're walking to Herbology when the class bully sticks out his foot and trips you. Do you...

a. Burst into tears and bury your face in the mud.
b. Consider cursing him but think better of it.
c. Start throwing punches — you're going to settle this with a Muggle duel!

2. The girl who's been tormenting you since you were a first-year is spreading a rumor that you're half troll. Do you...

a. Try to ignore your classmates' whispers and giggles but cry yourself to sleep.
b. Report her to a teacher.
c. Lock her in the bathroom with a full-grown mountain troll.

3. You're eating Pumpkin Pasties when a sneaky Slytherin performs a Switching Spell and suddenly there's a rat spleen in your mouth. Do you...

a. Continue chewing and pretend you didn't notice.
b. Spit it out and give that Slytherin your meanest glare.
c. Hex him until Professor McGonagall pries the wand from your fingers.

HOW DID YOU SCORE?

Spineless Sorcerer (mostly A's)
You're getting kicked around like a House-elf without a backbone. Wipe away those tears, grab a quill and start taking notes because you're about to get schooled in how to combat magical bullies.

Wishy-Washy Warlock (mostly B's)
You want to stick up for yourself but lack confidence. Get a few snappy comebacks under your belt and with a little bit of practice, you'll be telling off bullies before you know it!

Wand-Happy Wizard (mostly C's)
Whoa! Put down your fists, step away from your wand and take a deep breath. You need to learn how to deal with a bully in ways that won't land you in detention.

THE CHOSEN ONE

You must have a special birthday because the Prophecy has declared you the next Master of Insults! Get ready to spit comebacks the way a Hungarian Horntail spits fire. Use the insults on the following pages wisely, as you don't want to be expelled from Hogwarts for making a student unlock the Chamber of Secrets just to get away from you.

Practice makes perfect, so be sure to memorize your favorite comebacks to have at the ready! Furthermore, be careful not to use these insults on your younger siblings, or else your parents might send you a Howler and embarrass you in the Great Hall in front of your peers. Need a little insults practice? You might find it helpful to look into a mirror, say a few insults, and check to see if you're crying. If you are, you're doing it correctly! If you aren't, keep practicing, little wizard!

Insults can sometimes be overly powerful tools, so we've included some pages later in this handbook to help you escape precarious situations you might find yourself in, such as what to do if your comeback is so biting that a bully wants to physically harm you. Also, be prepared for surprise tests called R.A.T.s (Real-life Application Tests), which will challenge you to think on your feet and test the quickness of your magical wits. This book is here for you, and its pages are for your instruction so you'll be bullied no more!

SO WHAT ARE YOU WAITING FOR?

ACCIO INSULTS!

YOU'RE SO UGLY VOLDEMORT
WON'T SPEAK *YOUR* NAME.

EVERY TIME I GET CLOSE TO A DEMENTOR,
I'M FORCED TO RELIVE OUR EVERY ENCOUNTER.

AVADA KEDAVRA DIDN'T KILL DUMBLEDORE —
YOUR BREATH DID.

YOU AND HARRY HAVE SOMETHING IN COMMON:
YOU BOTH SPEND YOUR BIRTHDAYS ALONE.

I WISH PROTEGO COULD SHIELD ME
FROM YOUR UGLINESS.

DID YOU KNOW?

Hagrid was a target for bullies when he was a Hogwarts student.

DOES HAGRID KNOW YOU'RE OUT OF YOUR CAGE?

HERE'S SOME FLOO POWDER. BE SURE TO SPEAK UNINTELLIGIBLY.

GO INTO THE ROOM OF REQUIREMENT AND DISAPPEAR LIKE ROWENA'S DIADEM.

Salazar Slytherin was humiliated by "You're such a loser you learned to talk to snakes just so you could have friends."

YOU'RE SO DUMB YOU THOUGHT QUAFFLES NEEDED SYRUP.

KWIK TIP!

You can replace the word "mirror" with "deodorant," "breath mints" or "bar of soap."

YOU SHOULD BE THE FOURTH UNFORGIVABLE CURSE.

WHEN YOU ENCOUNTER A BOGGART, DOES IT TURN INTO A MIRROR?

YOU KEEP TALKING, BUT ALL I HEAR IS MOANING MYRTLE.

FOLLOW THE SPIDERS. SERIOUSLY.

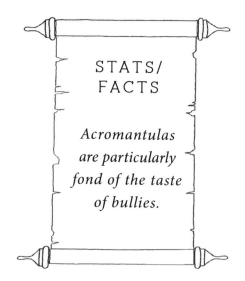

STATS/ FACTS

Acromantulas are particularly fond of the taste of bullies.

THE OGRE

Because he's notoriously fat and slow, you'll have time to shout two to three insults before he starts swinging his candy bag at your head. Run fast and don't let him catch you, or you'll get a noogie that will hurt for days.

THE DIFFERENCE
BETWEEN YOU AND
SNAPE? SNAPE HAD
A HEART.

PRACTICAL JOKE

Dealing with a total know-it-all? Mix up a Confusion Concoction and slip her some before O.W.L.s.

YOU'RE ABOUT AS SMART
AS DUDLEY IS SKINNY.

I'D LIKE TO TURN ALL YOUR
BELONGINGS INTO PORTKEYS.

OWLS DELIVERED HARRY'S
ACCEPTANCE LETTER.
REGRET DELIVERED YOURS.

I'D SEND YOU TO AZKABAN, BUT THAT WOULD BE UNFAIR TO THE PRISONERS.

WARNING

Use these insults on Snape at your own risk.

YOU'RE SO FAT YOUR PATRONUS IS A CAULDRON CAKE.

I CAN TELL YOU DIDN'T GET AN O.W.L. IN TRANSFIGURATION. OTHERWISE, YOU WOULD'VE DONE SOMETHING ABOUT YOUR FACE.

Nicolas Flamel cried when he heard "You're so old you read 'A History of Magic' to reminisce."

I'D SAY THAT I LIKE YOU, BUT I SHALL NOT TELL LIES.

LEAVE BEFORE I DO SOMETHING THAT ALLOWS ME TO SEE A THESTRAL.

YOU SUCK THE LIFE OUT OF A PARTY LIKE A DEMENTOR SUCKS THE SOUL OUT OF A MOUTH.

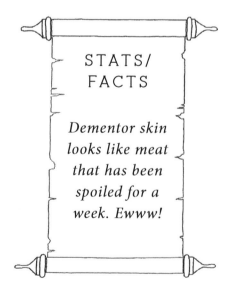

STATS/ FACTS

Dementor skin looks like meat that has been spoiled for a week. Ewww!

LET'S MAKE AN UNBREAKABLE VOW THAT YOU NEVER COME NEAR ME.

WHENEVER SOMEONE SAYS SOMETHING NICE ABOUT YOU, MY SNEAKOSCOPE STARTS WHISTLING.

WHEN I WALK PAST THE ROOM OF REQUIREMENT, I IMAGINE A ROOM WITHOUT YOU IN IT.

IF ONLY DEATH WOULD TAKE YOU AS HIS OWN.

DID YOU KNOW?

You can require a room where there are no bullies to be found.

R.A.T.S POP QUIZ
(REAL-LIFE APPLICATION TEST)

TEST 1: BANISHING THE BAD-MOUTHED BULLY

It's a beautiful day in Hogsmeade. Crimson leaves drift down from the trees and nestle on the thatched roofs of cottages and shops, and there's a slight chill to the air, announcing the arrival of autumn and the evening's Halloween Feast at Hogwarts. You enter Honeyduke's, debating whether to buy a Fizzing Whizbee or a Jelly Slug, when you notice a group of your classmates whispering and pointing in your direction. You glance over your shoulder and don't see anyone else. Yep, they're definitely talking about you.

The class bully saunters up to you, a sneer across his pinched face, and says, "I was just telling everyone that you don't need to wear a mask for Halloween. Your face is scary enough."

Your cheeks grow warm and your classmates' giggles echo in your ears, but you simply take a deep breath, shrug your shoulders and…

a. Hurl a Peppermint Toad at his head.

b. Say "When you encounter a Boggart, does it turn into a mirror?"

c. Run away and vow never to set foot in Hogsmeade again.

d. Hiss some indiscernible words and hope a venomous snake appears to do your bidding.

ANSWER: B

TOOLS OF THE MAGICAL TRADE

Sometimes a wizard needs a little help when trying to avoid a magical bully. The following list of tools will come in handy when you need to make it to class wedgie-free!

A WAND
A good wizard's last line of defense. Armed with this book, it's rare that you'll have to use it.

MARAUDER'S MAP
This is handy when avoiding bullying hot-spots such as behind the Herbology greenhouses or underneath the Quidditch bleachers.

INVISIBILITY CLOAK
Because this is extremely rare and valuable, we recommend arming yourself with insults from this book instead.

POLYJUICE POTION
Bullies are looking for you, so the safest way to make it to your classes is to change into someone else!

TIME-TURNER
Repair your reputation by traveling back in time to deliver that searing comeback!

FAMOUS BULLIES AND THE INSULTS THAT UNDID THEM

As you know, bullies have been around for as long as magic itself, and if you've been reading the Famous Wizard Insults cards scattered throughout these pages, then you're well aware that some of the greatest magical minds in history were the victims of painful pranks and humiliating hexes. But these witches and wizards aren't the only celebrity sorcerers who were tormented by bullies.

For instance, did you know…

- That Merlin wore that pointed hat to protect himself from swirlies?

- That Wendelin the Weird got so sick of hearing "your mum's so fat" jokes that she tried to be burned at the stake 47 times?

- That Agrippa was the first person — wizard or muggle — to receive a wedgie? (He quit wearing underwear with his toga after that.)

- That Dumbledore first broke his nose as a third-year when a Slytherin punched him for being a "muggle sympathizer"?

It's all true!

 *Keep reading those Famous Wizard Insults cards for more fascinating facts about magical bullying through the ages.

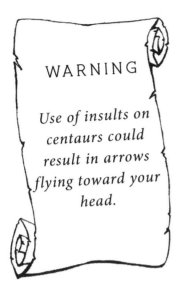
YOU'RE THE REASON MANDRAKES CRY.

IF VOLDEMORT WERE STILL AROUND, I'D TELL HIM YOU'RE THE CHOSEN ONE.

I SHOULD'VE TAKEN SOME FELIX FELICIS THIS MORNING. THEN MAYBE I WOULDN'T HAVE SEEN YOU TODAY.

Gellert Grindelwald cringed when he heard "You're so hideous you must have confused the Uglystick with the Deathstick."

AREN'T YOU ON THE COVER OF "THE MONSTER BOOK OF MONSTERS"?

I'D PUSH YOU INTO THE CABINET AT BORGIN AND BURKES IF I KNEW YOU WOULDN'T END UP BACK AT HOGWARTS.

WHO DRESSED YOU THIS MORNING? A HOUSE-ELF?

DID YOU KNOW?

The mistreatment of House-elves is a form of bullying. Join S.P.E.W. to make a difference!

PRACTICAL JOKE

Whip up a love potion for your nemesis and slip it into Millicent Bulstrode's pumpkin juice.

YOU DON'T EVER HAVE TO WORRY ABOUT SOMEONE SLIPPING YOU A LOVE POTION.

Snitches are for the Quidditch Field

When Malfoy cornered Harry in the halls of Hogwarts to insult him, Harry never ran off to tattle to Professor McGonagall. Instead, he stood his ground, looked Malfoy in the eye and defended himself with a smirk and a killer comeback! Malfoy had no choice but to walk away because he'd been bested by Harry's quick wit. This is a good example to follow — unless you're being physically harmed by someone. If that's the case, you should tell a professor and hope those bullies get detention with Umbridge. (Maybe they'll even have to carve "I shall not bully ever again" into the backs of their hands.)

But keep in mind that snitching when a bully calls you names — instead of retaliating with a witty remark — is an easy way to get singled out by a bully every day while walking to Herbology class. Try to insult the pants off that hooligan, but if that doesn't work, just turn and walk away. This is called "taking the high road" or "not stooping to the bully's level." Still, you have this book for a reason: to arm yourself with 101 insults that no bully can beat. With this book's help, you'll always walk away the victor. Meanwhile, your enemies will run to the loo and cry while a troll destroys the bathroom.

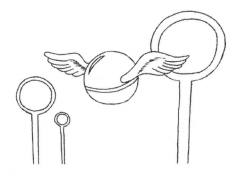

LUCIUS WAS RIGHT. DUMBLEDORE WILL
LET ANYONE IN HERE.

YOU'RE SO UGLY A DEMENTOR
WOULDN'T KISS YOU.

KWIK TIP!

You can replace "Dementor" with "Pansy Parkinson."

UNLESS THE PROPHECY SAYS
YOU'RE GOING TO WALK AWAY
RIGHT NOW, I DON'T WANT
TO HEAR IT.

HERE'S SOME POLYJUICE POTION.
GO TURN INTO SOMEONE ELSE.

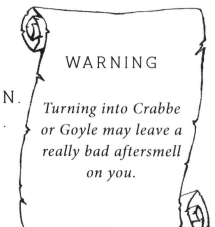

WARNING

Turning into Crabbe or Goyle may leave a really bad aftersmell on you.

Ptolemy puked when someone said to him "You're so stupid you thought the Sun orbited the Earth."

YOUR PERSONALITY IS WORSE THAN ALL SEVEN HORCRUXES.

SNAPE SENT AN OWL. HE WANTS HIS GREASY HAIR BACK.

SOMETIMES I SYMPATHIZE WITH SIRIUS' MOTHER. I'D WANT TO BLAST YOU OFF MY FAMILY TREE TOO.

YOU'RE SO UGLY HOGWARTS WAS NAMED AFTER YOU.

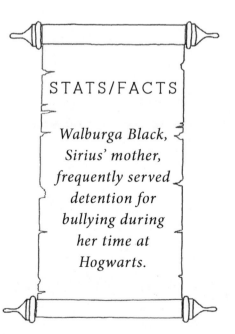

STATS/FACTS

Walburga Black, Sirius' mother, frequently served detention for bullying during her time at Hogwarts.

THE MEATHEAD

He's really big and super strong, and his wedgies are the worst by far. Sling insults at him to confuse him, but be sure to run away before he starts swinging his Beater's Bat at your face!

DID YOU KNOW?

Fred Weasley is rumored to have made up this insult about Cornelius Fudge.

YOU'RE SO FAT YOU TRIED TO EAT CORNELIUS FUDGE.

QUIETUS!

A FLOBBERWORM HAS MORE PERSONALITY THAN YOU.

IT'S A SHAME CEDRIC DIGGORY HAD TO DIE AND YOU'RE STILL HERE.

KWIK TIP!

You can replace this whole insult with "Your face reminds me of Flobberworm mucus."

HOW YOU BECAME A WIZARD IS ONE FOR THE DEPARTMENT OF MYSTERIES.

WHEN I LOOK INTO THE MIRROR OF ERISED, EVERYTHING IS THE SAME—YOU'RE JUST NOT THERE.

YOU'RE SO DUMB YOU JOINED THE DEATH EATERS BECAUSE YOU WERE HUNGRY.

IF YOU HAD A PHOENIX, IT WOULDN'T BOTHER WITH REBIRTH.

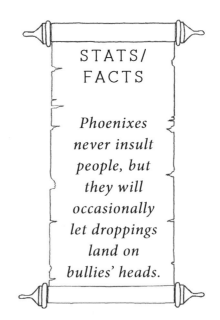

STATS/ FACTS

Phoenixes never insult people, but they will occasionally let droppings land on bullies' heads.

WARNING!

NEVER insult a Hippogriff unless you want a hoof to the face.

GO INSULT A HIPPOGRIFF.

YOUR FACE HAS THE SAME EFFECT ON ME AS A PUKING PASTILLE.

OLLIVANDER GAVE YOU A WAND TO MATCH YOUR HEAD: THICK AND HOLLOW.

KWIK TIP!

You can replace "thick and hollow" with "big and empty."

YOUR BUTT IS AS EXPLOSIVE AS A BLAST-ENDED SKREWT.

A LITTLE CHEEK CAN HAVE CONSEQUENCES

Delivering an insane insult can sometimes backfire. These killer come-backs could make your magical bully really mad — so mad he or she will want to use physical force against you. Remember when Malfoy cast Petrificus Totalus on Harry and stomped his face on the Hogwarts Express? That's something you want to avoid. Below you'll find a few scenarios to prepare for in the event bullies retaliate with muscle instead of their small brains.

THE WEDGIE

THE SWIRLIE

THE MAGIC CARPET RIDE

THE NOOGIE

THE ARM BURN

I ALSO GRAB MY FOREHEAD IN PAIN WHEN
I THINK OF YOU.

NO ONE BOTHERS FOLLOWING
YOU ON THE MARAUDER'S MAP.

YOU'RE SO UGLY THE MINISTRY OF MAGIC
THOUGHT YOU WERE AN UNREGISTERED ANIMAGUS.

I'D PLAY BEATER IF YOU
WERE THE BLUDGER.

PRACTICAL JOKE

*Disguise yourself as a
Ministry of Magic official
and ask your bully to fill
out an Animagus Registry
form.*

R.A.T.S POP QUIZ

(REAL-LIFE APPLICATION TEST)

TEST 2: QUICK COMEBACKS ON THE QUIDDITCH PITCH

You've spent the summer practicing Quidditch with your brother's hand-me-down broom and a bewitched golf ball, dodging imaginary Bludgers and catching that tiny ball every single time. You've even perfected the troublesome Wronski Feint, which, more often than not, resulted in a bloody nose. But the long hours of training and countless bloody handkerchiefs have paid off: You're the new Seeker on the House team — the youngest in nearly a century!

Now, the day of truth has arrived. It's the first Quidditch match of the season and your insides are writhing. (You feel rather like you've swallowed a couple of Cockroach Clusters and a handful of Gillyweed.) As you step onto the Quidditch pitch, you hear the cheers and jeers from your classmates, and then the opposing team's Seeker jabs you with his shoulder and knocks you to the ground. (Honestly, isn't he a little big to be playing Seeker?)

"I'd hate to see who else tried out for Seeker if you're the best your team has to offer," the brute sneers. Luckily, you're prepared for this. You square your shoulders, look that bully in the eye and...

a. Burst into tears and join Moaning Myrtle in the U-bend.

b. Say nothing and hope you'll catch the Snitch before he does.

c. Report him to Madam Hooch for teasing you.

d. Say "Well, I'd play Beater if you were the Bludger."

ANSWER: D

THE DOOFUS

Most of the insults you throw at him are over his head, but he's mean and gets a kick out of giving you arm burns. He laughs when the other bullies pick on you and likes to join in whenever he can. Attack his intelligence to send him packing! (But try to use small words so he'll understand.)

YOU'RE SO DUMB YOU THOUGHT THE DARK MARK WAS IN YOUR UNDERWEAR.

WHO SMELLS? YOU KNOW WHO.

EITHER SOMEONE DROPPED A DUNGBOMB OR YOU'RE STANDING TOO CLOSE TO ME.

YOU LOOK RIDDIKULUS!

STATS/FACTS

Boggarts hide in dark places because they are afraid of getting picked on.

ZONKO'S WAS FRESH OUT OF STINK PELLETS.
MIND IF I THROW YOU INSTEAD?

WHAT'S THAT IN YOUR
TEA LEAVES? PLEASE SAY
THE GRIM!

Tilly Toke said "Zonko's was fresh out of stink pellets. Mind if I throw you instead?" to Bridget Wenlock and then threw her into the Forbidden Forest. But Wenlock became pals with centaurs and got even.

THE BEST THING ABOUT
APPARATING? BEING ABLE
TO DISAPPEAR WHEN YOU
SHOW UP.

YOU'RE LIKE BERTIE BOTT'S EVERY FLAVOR BEANS
BECAUSE YOU LOOK LIKE VOMIT AND REMIND
ME OF BOOGERS.

R.A.T.S POP QUIZ
(REAL-LIFE APPLICATION TEST)

TEST 3: FORESEEING A BULLY-FREE FUTURE

Let's be honest, Divination has never been your best subject. You're talented in Transfiguration and you're a prodigy in Potions, but you can't seem to wrap your head around tea leaves and crystal balls. Plus, you've always been a bit on the clumsy side.

As you bend to retrieve your copy of "Unfogging The Future" from your bag during class, you knock your teacup to the floor, spilling the scalding liquid onto your foot and causing the table of girls beside you to collapse into giggles.

One of the girls — the one who's been tormenting you since you were a lowly first-year — leans over and whispers waspishly, "You know, when I look into my tea leaves, I see you failing this class and everyone realizing you're a squib."

That familiar pricking begins behind your eyes, but you force the tears back and without even a whisper of Accio, you summon all your courage and...

a. Take your seat and hope Professor Trelawney predicts her death next.

b. Ask Professor McGonagall if you can switch to second-period Muggle Studies.

c. Say "What's that in your tea leaves? Please say the Grim!"

d. Grab the nearest crystal ball and throw it at her.

ANSWER: C

THE PUNK

The Punk hides behind the Quidditch field bleachers waiting to punch your face in to the beat of Ramones songs. He may seem tough, but it's just an act — a well-delivered insult will make him face the music and get him off your back for good.

I WISH THE INVISIBILITY CLOAK WOULD MAKE YOU DISAPPEAR FOREVER.

THE SORTING HAT SHOULD'VE SORTED YOU INTO THE TRASH.

Alberta Toothill heard the insult "The Sorting Hat should've sorted you into the trash," and immediately jumped into the bin outside of Hagrid's Hut.

YOUR FACE BROKE COLIN CREEVEY'S CAMERA.

I BET IF YOU LOOKED A BASILISK IN THE EYE, IT WOULD DIE.

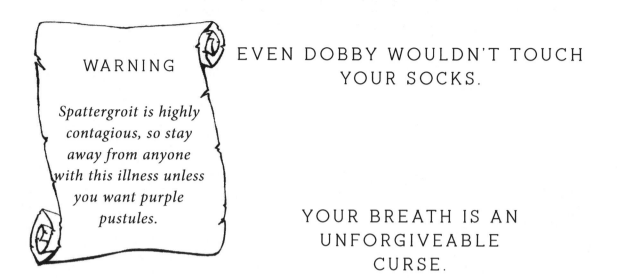

EVEN DOBBY WOULDN'T TOUCH YOUR SOCKS.

YOUR BREATH IS AN UNFORGIVEABLE CURSE.

DO YOU HAVE SPATTERGROIT OR DO YOU ALWAYS LOOK LIKE THAT?

THE ROOM OF REQUIREMENT WOULD JUST SUPPLY YOU WITH A PAPER BAG.

DID YOU KNOW?

The Room of Require-ment is a nice, quiet place to practice your comebacks.

IF I'D BEEN THE ONE TO LET YOU INTO HOGWARTS, I'D HAVE LET SNAPE KILL ME TOO.

WELL, I GUESS MY FLESH-EATING SLUG REPELLANT DOESN'T WORK.

I'VE MET SQUIBS WITH MORE TALENT.

DID YOU KNOW?

No one messed with squib Arabella Figg because she was quick with insults.

EVERY TIME I SEE YOU, I WANT TO DRINK FORGETFULNESS POTION.

GO SPLINCH YOURSELF.

KWIK TIP

You can also say "Get splinched."

IF I HAD A TIME-TURNER, I'D GO BACK TO BEFORE YOU EXISTED.

I WISH YOU WERE A HORCRUX. THAT WAY YOU'D BE DESTROYED BY NOW.

NOW I KNOW WHAT DUMBLEDORE MEANT ABOUT PITYING THE LIVING AND THOSE WITHOUT LOVE.

PRACTICAL JOKE

Draw a scar on your bully's head while he sleeps and leave a note saying Voldemort is coming for him.

THE SNOB

He insults you, your family and your pet Pygmy Puff — nothing is sacred! Plus, he always brags about his expensive clothes while laughing at your outfits with his cronies. Use witty insults against this guy to damage his pride.

YOU'RE SO UGLY, YOU COULD GET
A JOB AT GRINGOTTS.

ACCIO SHUT UP!

DID SOMEONE HIT YOU WITH
AN ENGORGEMENT CHARM?

SLYTHERIN SHOULD'VE
LOCKED YOU IN THE
CHAMBER OF SECRETS.

*Wilfred Elphick fled Little
Hangleton after Gifford
Ollerton shouted "Slytherin
should've locked YOU in the
Chamber of Secrets!" No
one's seen him since.*

THE SUBMARINE

This bully's favorite pastime is sitting on your chest and making you hit yourself. She even kicks your legs during Potions and flings newt eyes at you. She's slow but strong, so don't let her catch you and give you a swirlie.

PRACTICAL JOKE

Sprinkle some Wartcap Powder into the bully's bed, but be careful not to touch it!

YOU SHOULD TRY A LITTLE REPARO ON YOUR FACE.

IF YOU WERE A HOUSE-ELF, YOU'D HAVE NO PROBLEM GETTING CLOTHES.

YOU'RE WORSE THAN A DURSLEY.

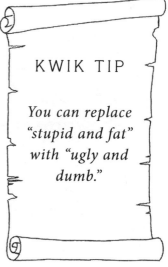

KWIK TIP

You can replace "stupid and fat" with "ugly and dumb."

YOUR WAND IS MADE OF STUPID AND FAT.

DID YOU KNOW?

Trolls smell like boiled cabbage and week-old socks.

THERE'S A TROLL HERE TO SEE YOU. HE WANTS HIS SMELL BACK.

YOU SHOULD GO TO ST. MUNGO'S. THERE'S SOMETHING WRONG WITH YOUR FACE.

NOT EVEN THE HUFFLEPUFFS WANT YOU.

YOU REMIND ME OF A HUNGARIAN HORNTAIL. YOUR BACK END IS AS TERRIBLE AS YOUR FRONT.

STATS/ FACTS

Hungarian Horntails are the biggest bullies at dragon school.

THE FRENEMY

She acts like a friend to your face, but the second you turn your back, she starts dissing you! She's incredibly vain, so insult her beauty to get her to stop talking smack.

KWIK TIP

You can replace the word "portraits" with "trolls," "Mandrakes" or "Howlers."

IF ONLY A SNITCH WOULD FLY INTO YOUR MOUTH EVERY TIME YOU OPENED IT.

I'VE HAD BETTER CONVERSATIONS WITH PORTRAITS.

YOU'D LOOK BETTER IF YOU JOINED THE HEADLESS HUNT.

PRACTICAL JOKE

Send Nearly Headless Nick to get your bully for the Headless Hunt in the middle of the night.

STARTING YOUR OWN INSULTS ARMY

An Insults Army could be just the type of club that other bullied witches and wizards at Hogwarts could use! Now that you're a master of the comeback, take your new knowledge and spread it to those who need it most. Sharing what you've learned not only helps others, but it also sends the bullies a powerful message: They no longer have power over you.

You have reclaimed your life so you can walk the halls of Hogwarts without worrying if The Punk or The Meathead will corner you and make you take a Magic Carpet Ride to Charms class. Furthermore, your Army can watch your back and help you if you find yourself cornered by a bully. Sometimes our minds go blank and we forget what to say in troubling times, but your club will always have your back!

There are many benefits to an Insults Army, but the biggest will be the friends and alliances you'll make by sharing your magical comebacks knowledge.

Accio Army!

> W.W.D.D.?
>
> *What would Dumbledore do? Offer help to those who need it at Hogwarts.*

INSULTS TO MAKE
ALL MAGICAL BULLIES CRY

IF QUIRRELL HAD BEEN CURSING YOU, NO ONE
WOULD'VE INTERRUPTED HIS CONCENTRATION.

WHAT DID YOU SAY? I'M SORRY.
I DON'T SPEAK TROLL.

EVERY TIME YOU SPEAK IT FEELS LIKE
YOU'VE CAST CRUCIO ON ME.

YOU'RE SO FAT THE SORTING HAT SHOULD'VE
PLACED YOU IN ALL FOUR HOUSES.

THE WIZARD WHO LIVED

You've read up on proper comeback delivery, learned the tricks of the trade and committed 101 magical insults to memory*. You're well aware of the magical bullying threats out there and have armed yourself accordingly. You've even faced down a bully in Hogsmeade, told off a tormentor on the Quidditch field and informed that fortune-telling troublemaker that she won't be picking on you in the near future.

After observing your progress, the Wizarding Examinations Authority has decided to award you full marks on your R.A.T.s.

CONGRATULATIONS!

You're now ready to face any bully** that comes your way — magical or not. Now go out there and live a bully-free life, little wizard!

*Or you've at least read them.

**But just in case things ever get out of hand, it's best to have a few jinxes up your sleeve. We recommend the Bat-Bogey Hex. It's just gross.

CONJURE UP YOUR OWN INSULTS!

Did you think of some great insults that weren't included in this book? Write them down here! Crushing comebacks should be infinite, so come up with as many as your magical heart desires.

MISCHIEF MANAGED.

ABOUT THE AUTHORS

BIRDY JONES, a Ravenclaw who represented her house in the Triwizard Tournament, is a video producer for the Mother Nature Network. She has a master's degree in video production from DePaul University and has used her magic to self-publish two children's books. She also writes middle-grade and young-adult novels, and she enjoys tricking her friends into eating the gross flavors of Bertie Bott's Every Flavor Beans. *www.birdyjones.wordpress.com*

LAURA J. MOSS, a Gryffindor who played Chaser for her house Quidditch team, is an editor for the Mother Nature Network. She has a master's degree in journalism from the University of South Carolina and her articles have appeared on CNN.com, The Huffington Post, Forbes.com and Yahoo.com. She also writes young-adult novels and enjoys baking homemade Pumpkin Pasties. *www.laurajmoss.com*

Made in the USA
Lexington, KY
09 October 2017